Samplers from A to Z

SAMPLERS *from A to Z*

Pamela A. Parmal

BOSTON

MFA Publications

a division of the

Museum of Fine Arts, Boston

MFA Publications
a division of the Museum of Fine Arts, Boston
295 Huntington Avenue
Boston, Massachusetts 02115

Published in conjunction with the exhibition
"Common Threads: A Showcase of Samplers,"
organized by the Museum of Fine Arts, Boston,
from March 29, 2000, to July 23, 2000.

Support for this book was provided by the
Andrew W. Mellon Publications Fund.

Cover: Maria Jesus de Gambaza, Mexican, Puebla,
Sampler (detail), 1832 (p. 34)

Frontispiece: Artist Unknown, Probably German,
Band Sampler (detail), early 1800s (p. 62)

Page 7: Artist Unkown, German, *Sampler* (detail),
1692 (p. 42)

Designed by Cynthia Rockwell Randall
Printed by Sawyer Printers, Charlestown, MA

Available through D.A.P./Distributed Art Publishers
155 Sixth Avenue, 2nd floor
New York, NY 10013
Tel. (212) 627-1999   Fax (212) 627-9484

FIRST EDITION
Printed and bound in the United States of America

Foreword

In 1877, an eighteenth-century sampler by the Boston schoolgirl Ann Wing became the first piece of needlework to enter the Museum's collection. Ann Wing's sampler, with its finely embroidered alphabet, religious verses, and floral borders, set a high standard for future acquisitions. Since then, the Museum's collection of samplers has grown to over three hundred; as may be seen from the examples chosen for this book, many of those acquisitions have risen to the standard set over one hundred years ago.

The quality of the collection is largely due to the generosity and discernment of the Museum's many donors. Special acknowledgment goes to Mrs. Arthur Croft, who donated the Gardner Brewer Collection that included many fine South German samplers; Mr. Philip Lehman, who gave the Museum his wife's important collection of embroidery and textiles; and finally Miss Elizabeth Day McCormick who, through her gift of over four thousand textiles and costumes, made the Museum of Fine Arts's textile collection one of the most important in the world.

We are extremely grateful to the Historic Needlework Guild and the Mellon Foundation for making this book possible through their generous donations. Pamela Parmal, Curator of Textiles and Costumes, diligently worked through the alphabet selecting samplers for publication, while the staff of the Gabriella and Leo Beranek Textile Conservation Laboratory prepared them for photography. This book is the first Museum publication in which digital photographs have been used exclusively, and we would like to thank the Ladies Committee of the Museum of Fine Arts for supporting the purchase of the camera used to take these pictures. The Museum staff involved in this pioneering effort also include: Mark Polizzotti, the Museum's Publisher and editor of this book; Cynthia Randall, its designer; Nancy Allen, Director of Information Resources; Thomas Lang, Director of Photographic Resources; and finally John Woolf, Digital Imaging and Photography Specialist, whose magnificent images have brought out the best in each sampler.

MALCOLM ROGERS
Ann and Graham Gund Director of the Museum of Fine Arts, Boston

Introduction

Alphabets, floral borders, and cross stitch are the first things most people think of when they hear the word *sampler*. But the image of schoolgirl embroidery, while a part of sampler history, is not the whole story. Samplers have existed since at least the thirteenth century, when professional Egyptian embroiderers used them as prototypes for their clients. Amateur needleworkers throughout Europe made samplers to record stitches and patterns and, by the seventeenth century, they were finally incorporated into a girl's school curriculum. As the use of samplers in education spread, girls progressed from embroidered examples to more complicated lace, darning, whitework, and knitting, while map and almanac samplers introduced even more variety. This book, primarily written as an introduction to samplers and their history, is also an exploration of their geographic, cultural, and technical diversity.

The earliest sampler in the Museum of Fine Art's collection, a fragment from Mamluk Egypt dated between the fourteenth and fifteenth centuries, takes us as far back into sampler history as we can now go (see O, p. 40). The Mamluks ruled Egypt and Syria from 1250 to 1517. During this period, a thriving industry for embroidered household linens and clothing existed in the bazaars. Geometric borders were worked onto linen shifts and sashes covering seams and edging hems. The Mamluks, who worked primarily in darning stitch, favored borders with interlacing bands, zig-zags, and repetitive S scrolls, patterns similar to those found on textiles and embroideries made throughout the Mediterranean region.

By the end of the fifteenth century, a fashion for linen embroidered with similar borders spread throughout Europe, from Italy into the courts of Henry IV of France and of Tudor England. The first evidence we find for the making of embroidered samplers in Europe comes from this period. Although no known examples survive, a painting by the Flemish artist Joos van Cleve (about 1485–1540) contains the earliest depiction of a European sampler: a folded linen spot sampler sitting on a table in front of the Virgin and Child (see S, p. 48).[1] Embroidered onto the cloth are small geometric floral stems, similar to ones found on the fashionable smocks worn in Northern Europe in the mid-sixteenth century.[2] Samplers like this one were probably made by amateur needlewomen to collect stitches and designs for future reference.

Along with the evidence provided in the van Cleve painting, the historian Averil Colby has located many written references to sixteenth-century samplers. These references indicate that their use—both to collect patterns and stitches and to teach young girls needlework skills—was fairly well established by the first quarter of the century.[3] Colby's research also shows that samplers played an ambiguous role in women's lives: for some, they were a tool in a girl's education, while others saw them as symbols of the "silken follies" on which women wasted their time.[4]

Although the education of seventeenth-century girls of the middle and upper classes is not well documented, their samplers are tangible evidence of its formalization. Though the spot sampler continued to be worked throughout the century, it was eventually supplanted by the band sampler with its more organized format (see B, p. 14). In Britain, single band samplers were common, while on the Continent, German, Italian, and Spanish teachers preferred double, triple, or even quadruple bands. Schoolgirls embroidered samplers with neat rows of repetitive polychrome silk and whitework borders (see W, p. 56; I, p. 28; and J, p. 30). The patterns and stitches used had their origins in the borders embroidered onto sixteenth-century linens. Although previously fashionable, the designs no longer related to contemporary clothing ornament and are an indication that the sampler's role as a design reference diminished as it became a tool for education.

As the sampler became a standard aspect of the formal female curriculum, it further adapted itself to its new role. The addition of the alphabet and numbers to samplers in the seventeenth century, while providing students with the practical skills necessary to mark linen (see A, p. 12), may also have reflected the increasing emphasis on literacy brought about by the Protestant Reformation and Luther's doctrine of the "priesthood of all believers."[5] Luther believed that all men and women should be able to read the Bible, and the Protestants encouraged parents either to teach their children to read within the home or to send them to school.

From the sixteenth to the eighteenth century, the most common tool used to teach reading was the hornbook. It was made of a wooden frame onto which a sheet of parchment or paper was sandwiched with a transparent sheet of horn.

The alphabet, both upper and lower case, was written or printed across the first rows of the paper. Vowels appeared in the next row and were followed by a table of vowels combined with consonants. The hornbook usually finished with the Lord's Prayer. Pointing to the appropriate line of the horn book, the teacher taught reading by first pronouncing syllables, then saying words, and finally reading sentences and verses. Whether or not the sampler was actually used like a hornbook to teach girls to read is unclear, but at very least it would have familiarized them with the alphabet and with how letters could be combined to create their name, a date, and Biblical or other verses.

By the end of the seventeenth century, samplers again evolved to meet the changing needs of education. Teachers in continental Europe continued to emphasize fine needlework skills through a range of stitches and designs, while in Great Britain, the sampler's role in the moral education of young girls appears to have taken prominence. In the eighteenth century, the number of stitches and complex patterns found on British samplers declined, as the inclusion of Bible verses and moral sayings increased. This reflected the educational practices of the period, when it was believed that children learned best through repetition and memorization (see V, p. 54). The form of the sampler also changed as it evolved further away from its origins as a needleworker's reference tool and became tangible evidence of a girl's education and accomplishments. The band sampler, with its orderly rows of repetitive patterns, gave way to a squarer format, with a more pictorial, symmetric design. Borders around all four edges of the sampler were more common, and they often enclosed moral sayings or a verse from the Bible.

The British colonists brought their sampler traditions with them when they settled in the New World. The few seventeenth-century American samplers that have survived are almost indistinguishable from those of Great Britain, with stylized floral bands, alphabets, and moral verses (see Q, p. 44). This continuity is the result of sampler traditions being transferred from instructor to student, as it was the teacher who often designed and laid out her pupil's work. Some teachers reinterpreted the design of the samplers they had embroidered as young girls, creating their own unique styles. In this way groups of similar samplers can be identified with a specific time, place, or even instructor.

The continuity and innovation between British and American samplers can be seen in several examples illustrated in this book. The design of the sampler embroidered by British schoolgirl Elizabeth Steell (see G, p. 24) appears to be a model type that influenced at least two American examples: one by Betsy Davis (see R, p. 46), the other by Rebecah French (see A, p. 12). Elizabeth Steell made her pictorial sampler in 1721; she embroidered Chapter xx from Exodus on a double tablet surrounded by a floral border on three sides and religious imagery at the top. At the center of the bottom border is a pot out of which an elaborate floral vine grows, while at the bottom of the side borders are two vases with flowers. The use of vases with floral vines appears to have been quite popular with American needleworkers. Betsy Davis worked into her sampler floral side borders that grow out of two vases similar to those of Elizabeth Steell, while Rebecah French's sampler is dominated by a pot with flowers at the bottom center. Betsy's work is typical of the samplers produced under the Providence schoolteacher Mary Balch's tutelage, while Rebecah's is identified with samplers produced in Canterbury, New Hampshire.

As the eighteenth century progressed, the movement toward more pictorial needlework continued, and embroidered pictures, not the sampler, became the ultimate achievement for a well-educated young lady of means. Meanwhile, with education becoming more widespread among the lower classes, the practical applications of the sampler were again valued. One of the aims in education was to teach girls a skill that they could then use to help support themselves. During the eighteenth and nineteenth centuries, a variety of sampler types evolved in which students learned more utilitarian aspects of needlework. Embroidery samplers highlighted the practical uses of embroidery, such as marking linen and plain sewing, while other kinds of samplers were developed that used darning, whitework, holliepoint, and knitting (see D, p. 18; W, p. 56; H, p. 26; K, p. 32).

With the education reforms of the late nineteenth century, samplers no longer had a place in the classroom, except in orphanages and charity schools where they were still used to teach girls a trade. Even as the sampler went out of fashion in the classroom, however, a growing appreciation for embroidery brought about by the Arts and Crafts and Colonial Revival movements of the later nineteenth and early twentieth centuries rekindled interest in historic samplers. Embroidery guilds were founded, sparking a new interest in early needlework. Collectors turned their attention to samplers and, eventually, important examples found their way into museums. How surprised the embroiderers, needlewomen, and schoolgirls who created the samplers in this book would have been to see the audience that now exists for their cherished handiwork!

1. Van Cleve's *The Holy Family* is in the collection of the Currier Gallery of Art, Manchester, New Hampshire.
2. Margaret Abegg, *Apropos Patterns* (Bern: Abegg-Stiftung, 1978), 17, fig. 2.
3. Averil Colby, *Samplers*, 2nd ed. (London: B. T. Batsford Ltd., 1984), 143–47.
4. Ibid., 155.
5. John D. Pulliam, *History of Education in America*, 4th ed. (Columbus, Ohio: Merrill Publishing Company, 1987), 10.

Alphabet

By the seventeenth century, the alphabet had become a standard feature of schoolgirl samplers. Its inclusion had a two-fold purpose. Along with familiarizing students with the letters of the alphabet, their name, and the rudiments of spelling, it also introduced them to the techniques used for marking linen. Because household and personal linens were sent out for laundering or done in huge batches, it was necessary to number and mark them with the owner's initials to ensure their proper return. As such, only the most legible forms of stitching were used. This sampler, worked by Rebecah French about 1811, contains three alphabets worked in cross, eyelet, and satin stitches. The first alphabet, called "round hand," was the hand most often used in eighteenth-century commercial documents. It was also called "school hand" because it was the first script taught to students.

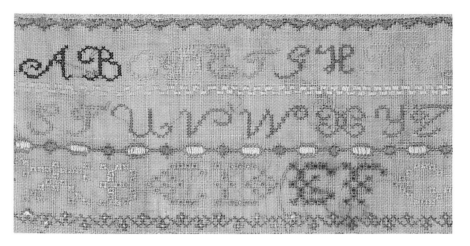

Rebecah French

American, New Hampshire, born 1802

Sampler, about 1811
19⅞ x 17¹¹⁄₁₆ in. (50.5 x 45 cm)
Plain weave linen embroidered with silk
Stitches: cross, eyelet, satin, sawtooth, stem, and tent
Bequest of Dorothy M. Sneath 60.167

13

Band Sampler

The band sampler, characterized by horizontal rows of needlework designs, probably developed alongside the fifteenth-century fashion for embroidered borders on household and personal linens. Embroiderers collected border designs from friends, pattern books, or any available source and worked them onto linen samplers to preserve them for later reference. The earliest dated band samplers, from Germany and Great Britain, contain rows of patterns in both whitework (see W, p.56) and double-running stitch. Both techniques were used on personal linens at the end of the sixteenth and early seventeenth centuries.

As the sampler was incorporated into formal education during the seventeenth century, it gradually lost its function as a repertoire of stitches and patterns and evolved into a tool for introducing girls to basic literacy and needlework skills. The neat, well-organized appearance of the band sampler suited its new role. By the middle of the century, when Hannah Thornbush embroidered her sampler, the patterns she chose no longer related to fashionable dress but were used to showcase her abilities. As the century progressed, the alphabet, the girl's name, and a date were embroidered onto samplers and, by the end of the century, religious or instructional verses were also included.

Hannah Thornbush
British

Band Sampler, mid-1600s
33¼ x 7⅜ in. (84.5 x 18.7 cm)
Plain weave linen embroidered with silk
Stitches: couching, cross, detached buttonhole (speckled), double running, eyelet, long-armed cross, marking cross, Montenegrin cross, running, and satin
The Elizabeth Day McCormick Collection
43.278

Artist Unknown

British or Continental European

Berlinwork Sampler, 1840s
30⅛ x 10⅛ in. (76.5 x 25.7 cm)
Plain weave cotton embroidered in silk and wool
Stitches: cross, plush, satin, and tent; pulled work
The Elizabeth Day McCormick Collection
43.984

Canvaswork

Canvaswork refers to embroidery worked on a balanced plain-weave ground, with the stitches placed by counting the threads of the fabric. While this gives a less naturalistic look to the embroidery (because the stitches follow the rigid geometry of the woven cloth), the regularity of the ground fabric provides a more manageable surface on which to master needlework skills. For this reason, canvaswork formed the basis for the schoolgirl embroidery curriculum.

During the nineteenth century, canvaswork known as "Berlinwork" became the most popular form of amateur embroidery. Berlinwork embroideries were based on cheaply printed colored charts. The first patterns were printed in Berlin in the early nineteenth century and most often worked with colorful wool yarns produced in Germany. The Berlinwork sampler shown here is embroidered primarily in tent stitch, though it also includes less typical stitches, such as plush, cross, satin, and pulled work. The sampler was probably made during the 1840s, when a fashion for imitating black lace in Berlinwork arose. A narrow band of black pulled work was embroidered between the rows of plush stitches. During this same period, birds also became popular subjects for Berlinwork patterns, inspired by the publication of John James Audubon's *Birds of America* (1823–38), John Gould's *Birds of Australia* (1833–35), and other books on natural history.

Darning

Darning, which involved interweaving new threads into the warp and weft of a cloth to patch holes and tears, was an important skill for a household embroiderer to acquire. This was especially true prior to the mid-nineteenth century, when advancements in spinning and weaving technology made textiles more affordable. Darning samplers first became popular in Northern Europe during the early eighteenth century, then spread to Great Britain and the United States.

Darning samplers usually included several repairs. Squares were cut out of the ground material and each darned in a different weave structure. One of the signs of a good darn was maintaining a similar tension between the inserted yarns and the original warp and weft so as not to create buckling or pulling. The original embroiderer of this sampler showed remarkable skill, which is made more obvious when compared with a subsequent repair in the upper left corner. Someone has redarned a cut square by introducing yellow silk yarns into the weft; the repair was put in under too much tension, distorting the ground fabric.

F. R. Richtrigt
Dutch

Darning sampler, 1813
21⅛ x 21⅛ in. (53.7 x 53.7 cm)
Plain weave linen embroidered with silk and linen
Stitches: eyelet, marking cross, and two-sided Italian cross; simple darning and pattern darning
The Elizabeth Day McCormick Collection
43.954

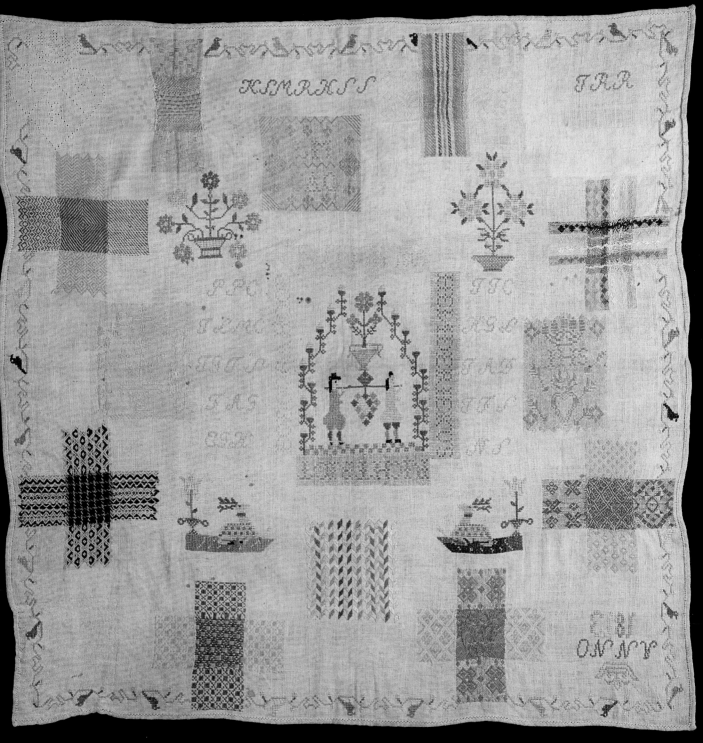

Embroidery

Technically speaking, embroidery is the art of ornamenting cloth and other fabrics with needlework figures. Of course, the use of ornamentation goes beyond needlework to all aspects of life. But in terms of textiles, evidence of embroidery goes back to at least the mid-fourteenth century B.C.E., with an elaborately embroidered shirt in the tomb of Egypt's King Tutankhamen. The craft could well go back 45,000 years, as suggested by needles excavated from a Chinese archaeological site. The urge to embellish can also be seen in the evolution of sampler design. By the early nineteenth century, girls were no longer content with repeating the alphabet, numbers, and decorative bands, and were taking samplers to their fullest pictorial possibilities, creating images such as this country scene that Ann Folwill made in 1804.

Ann Folwill
American, Burlington, New Jersey

Pictorial Sampler, 1804
17½ x 12½ in. (44.4 x 31.8 cm)
Plain weave linen embroidered with silk and
metallic thread
Stitches: chain, couching, cross, running,
satin (speckled), sawtooth, and split
Bequest of Edna H. Howe 54.1575

French knot

The French knot is made by pulling the needle through the back of the cloth to the front, wrapping the thread around the needle, inserting it back through the ground cloth, and pulling it tight. Knots are often used to give variety and texture to the surface of an embroidery, and are sometimes the primary source of ornament. The embroiderer of this sampler has stitched regularly spaced knots to create the kind of ornamental borders often found on seventeenth-century samplers but worked in double running stitch or pulled work. Where this type of sampler originated is not known, but most likely it came from South Germany: some of the polychrome cross stitch motifs visible at the bottom—such as the two-handled vase with flowers, the wreath enclosing the embroiderer's initials and date, and the small apple and pear—are similar to others found in well documented South German samplers.

Artist Unknown
Probably South German

Band Sampler, 1733
34 x 7½ in (86.4 x 19.1 cm)
Plain weave linen embroidered with linen and silk
Stitches: chain border stitch and variation, composite stitch, cross, feather, French knots, and long-armed cross
Bequest of Mrs. Arthur Croft, "Gardner Brewer Collection" 01.6275

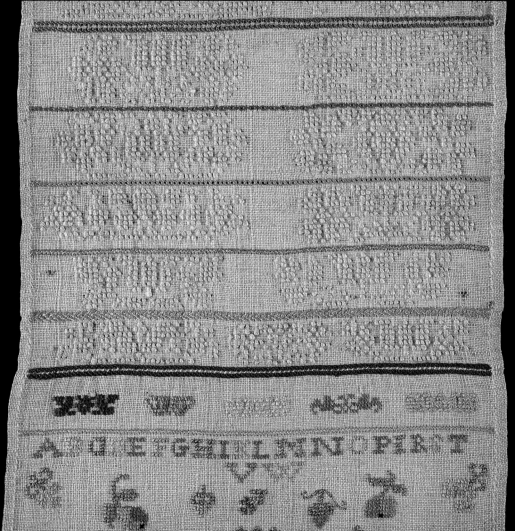

ABCDEFGHIJLMNOPRST
VW

Gold

Gold is found in the prestigious cloth of most cultures. The Greeks incorporated gold beads into their weaving, the Japanese stenciled gold leaf onto silk, and eighteenth-century Europeans wove with complex gold yarns having flat, kinky, or cork-screw surfaces. Gold not only added to the value of the cloth, but enlivened it with glimmers that would have been splendid in candlelight or torchlight.

Elizabeth Steell, who embroidered this sampler in 1721, incorporated metallic yarn into her work. The metal yarns are embroidered in low relief, a technique used often on eighteenth-century men's suits and women's accessories. Women's aprons and stomachers embroidered with flowers and vases similar to those found on Elizabeth Steell's sampler were popular during the early part of the century. They are generally believed to have been professional work, but this sampler shows that a young woman could well have embroidered her own.

Elizabeth Steell
British

Sampler, 1721
17⅞ x 14¹¹⁄₁₆ in. (45.5 x 37.3 cm)
Plain weave linen embroidered with silk and metallic thread
Stitches: Bullion knots, chain, couching, cross, French knots, florentine, satin, stem, and tent; metallic thread embroidered in couching, couching over string, and laid work
The Elizabeth Day McCormick Collection
43.285

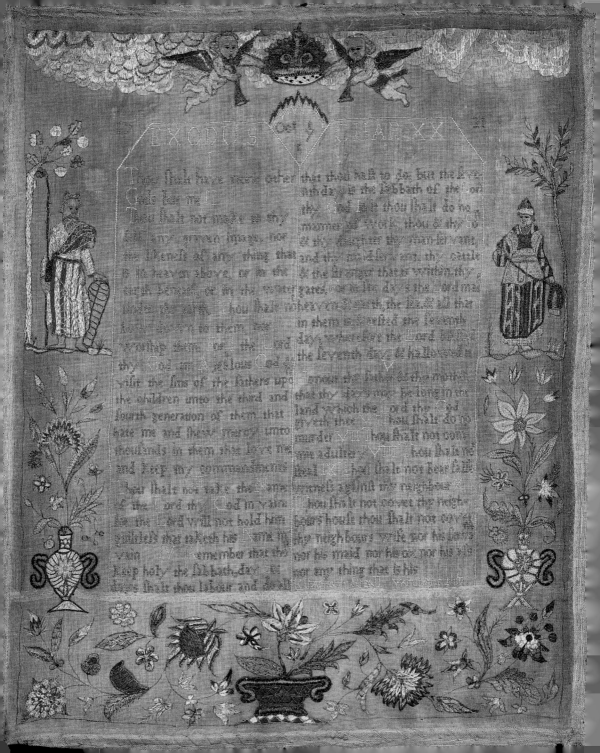

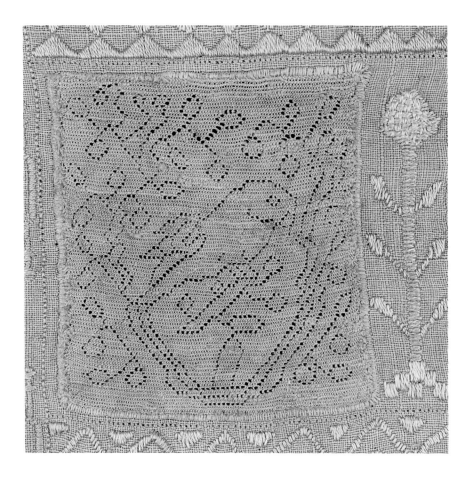

Holliepoint sampler

Holliepoint refers to a distinctly British version of needle lace in which small open areas are left in a section of densely packed buttonhole stitches to create a pattern. Developed in the seventeenth century, holliepoint was used during the eighteenth on baby clothes and christening sets. The technique appears to have been especially popular during the 1720s and 1730s, and again during the 1760s. This sampler, which Sarah Leesley embroidered in 1739, shares many similarities with other holliepoint samplers of similar date. Along with squares and circles filled with holliepoint, others of *reticella* (see I, p. 28) can be found surrounded by borders embroidered in satin stitch. Sarah Leesley's sampler is almost identical to another from the same year by Mary Tredwell (Victoria & Albert Museum).

Sarah Leesley
British

Holliepoint sampler, 1739
8⅞ x 8¾ in. (22.5 x 22.2 cm)
Plain weave linen embroidered with linen and silk
Stitches: needle weaving, reverse chain, satin, and sawtooth; cutwork with buttonhole, knotted buttonhole, and buttonhole filling
Gift of Philip Lehman in memory of his wife, Carrie L. Lehman 38.1137

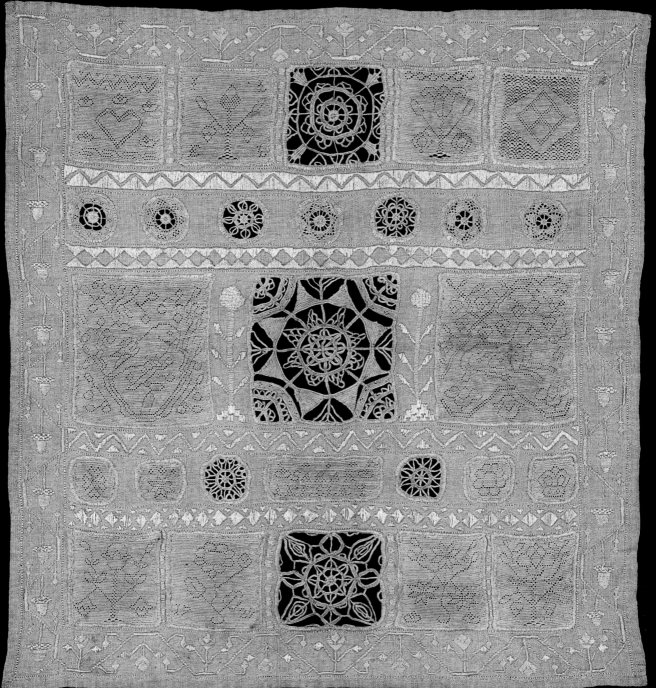

Artist Unknown
British

Sampler, 1656
20⅝ x 7 in. (52.4 x 17.8 cm)
Plain weave linen embroidered with linen
Stitches: double running, satin, and stem;
pulled work with double hem, four-sided,
and hem; cutwork with buttonhole and
detached buttonhole
Gift of Mrs. Samuel Cabot 35.2000

Italian cutwork

Italian cutwork (*punto tagliato*) developed during the sixteenth century.
However, Italy was not the only place in
which fashionable cutwork was made;
centers sprang up throughout Europe,
notably in Flanders, Germany, and
France. In the sixteenth century, the
term *cutwork* was applied to embroidery
in which parts of the ground were cut
away and filled with needlelace. It was
especially popular in the ornamentation of linens. The large open grid,
filled with delicate tracery, made an ele-
gant edging for ruffs, cuffs, and hand-
kerchiefs, and was later used to make
the large standing collars that became
popular about 1610. Cutwork went out
of fashion by the second quarter of the
seventeenth century, when free-form
bobbin and needle laces came into
their own. However, it lived on in
schoolgirl samplers such as this one.

   After the completion of a silk band
sampler (see B, p. 14), a British schoolgirl would execute a second in whitework. The girl who created this sampler
combined satin stitch borders with a
type of cutwork known as *reticella.*
Reticella is worked by cutting squares
out of the ground cloth and leaving a
grid of warp and weft yarns. The
squares are filled in using buttonhole
stitch to build a delicate pattern similar
to Gothic tracery. In this sampler, the
top band of *reticella* has a distinctly
English character, with three-dimen-
sional thistle buds attached to the
central square.

J

Artist Unknown
British

Sampler, about 1650–1675
25 ⁹⁄₁₆ x 7 in. (64.3 x 17.9 cm)
Plain weave linen embroidered with linen,
silk, and metallic thread
Stitches: bullion, double hem, and satin; cutwork with buttonhole fillings and hem stitch
Elizabeth Day McCormick Collection
43.272

Judith and Holofernes

The top band of this sampler contains
a rare example of polychrome cutwork
(see I, p. 28). Depicted on the band is
the story of Judith and Holofernes, one of
many biblical tales embroidered by seventeenth-century schoolgirls. In this sampler, the needleworker has chosen to por-
tray three scenes from the story. On the
far left is the corpse of the Assyrian general Holofernes, who laid siege to the widow
Judith's city of Bethusia. In the center are
Judith and her serving woman holding
the general's head. Judith entered the
camp of the Assyrians and tricked them
into believing she had betrayed her people. After a drunken banquet Judith was
left alone with Holofernes, who intended
to seduce her; but overcome by wine he
fell asleep, opening the way for his death.
In the final scene, Holofernes's head sits
on the wall of Bethusia, which the
Assyrians quickly abandoned. This grue-
some tale, seemingly inappropriate for a
young girl, was in fact interpreted as an
expression of good triumphing over evil,
while Judith was seen as a virtuous woman
for not succumbing to Holofernes.

This whitework sampler illustrates the
embroiderer's progression, from the less
demanding pulled work band at the bottom through increasingly complicated
cutwork bands with needlelace fillings.
In the second band from the top, the
ground fabric has been completely cut
away and filled with a freeform needlelace
design more typical of the fashionable
lace of the mid-seventeenth century.

Knitting sampler

Knitting samplers, like whitework, darning, and marking, had very practical applications within the household. Stockings, caps, gloves, and other accessories were often knit in the home when time permitted. Although the knit lace bands of this sampler appear to have nothing to do with practicality, they were a very popular element of early nineteenth-century stockings. Lace designs with vertical patterns were knit into the front of stockings at the ankle and higher, and would have been visible under the slightly raised hemlines of the 1820s and 1830s. The sampler is generally identified as German, but its true date and origin are unknown.

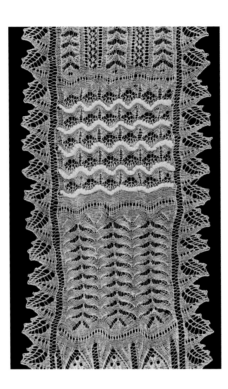

Maria Jesus de Gambaza
Mexican, Puebla

Sampler, 1832
29⅛ x 23 in. (74 x 58.5 cm)
Plain weave linen embroidered with silk
and cotton
Stitches: eyelet, French knot, shaded satin,
satin (speckled), and stem; cutwork with
detached buttonhole stitch
The Elizabeth Day McCormick Collection
46.764

Landscape

By the eighteenth century, schoolgirl samplers were no longer rolled up and stored in work boxes, but became pictures in their own right, to be framed and hung proudly in a girl's home. The format of samplers changed to suit their new role. Pictorial imagery began to dominate and the organization became more symmetric. Landscapes, for the most part inspired by print sources, found their way into samplers. This visual and technical *tour de force* is made up of elements that would have allowed the student to practice her silk embroidery and whitework skills; but by organizing them symmetrically and choosing such pictorial images, Maria Jesus de Gambaza has created a testimony to her education and accomplishments. At the top of the sampler she has acknowledged her teachers, explaining that she began her work under the direction of Doña Nicolaza Invera (who passed away during its execution) and finished it with Doña Guadalupe del Corral.

Map sampler

The stitching of map samplers began in the eighteenth century, when school curriculums broadened to emphasize more practical subjects such as mathematics, geography, civics, and the natural sciences. To aid in the study of geography, girls created map samplers. Teachers would draw the boundaries of the chosen geographical regions— the two hemispheres, continental Europe, Great Britain, and Africa were favorites—and the students would stitch in national boundaries, towns and villages, rivers, mountains, and seas. As map samplers became more popular, they were printed commercially. The maps of the eastern and western hemispheres on which these embroideries are based probably appeared in a now unidentified geography text.

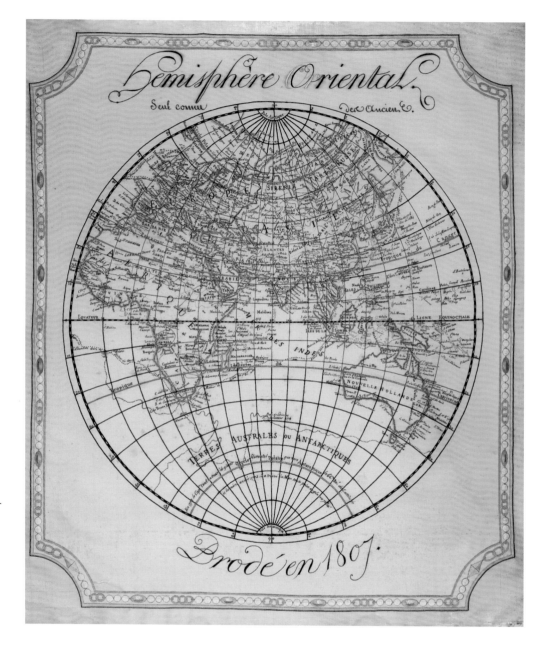

Artist Unknown

French

Hémisphère Oriental seul connu des Ancien E., 1807

29⅜ x 26¼ in. (74.6 x 66.7 cm)

Plain weave silk embroidered with silk

Stitches: back, chain, couching, French knot, running, satin, shaded satin, split, and stem

The Elizabeth Day McCormick Collection 44.466

Artist Unknown

French

Hémisphère Occidental ou Nouveau Monde découvert en 1492, 1807

31⅝ x 26¼ in. (80.3 x 66.7 cm)

Plain weave silk embroidered with silk

Stitches: back, chain, couching, French knot, running, satin, shaded satin, split, and stem

The Elizabeth Day McCormick Collection 44.465

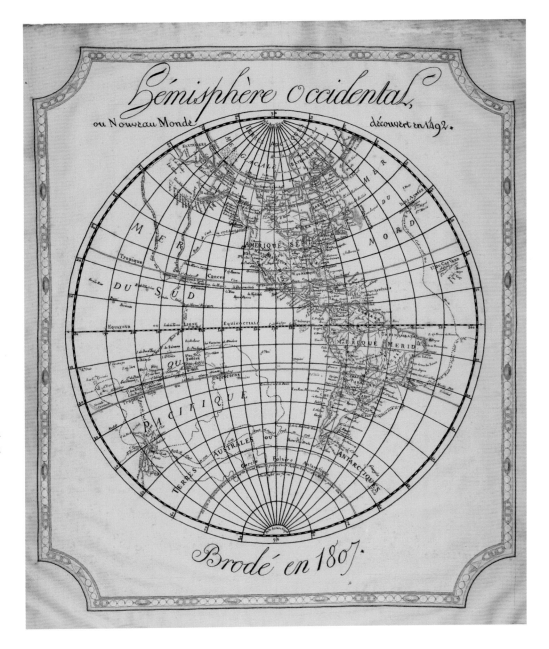

Artist Unkown
South German

Sampler, 1737
15 ⁹⁄₁₆ x 12 ½ in. (40.2 x 31.7 cm)
Plain weave linen embroidered with silk
and metallic thread
Stitches: couching, cross, French knot, marking cross, satin, shaded satin and stem;
canvas work stitches including florentine,
rococo, and tent
Bequest of Mrs. Arthur Croft, "Gardiner
Brewer Collection" 01.6271

Numbers

Embroidered along the top edge of this sampler are the alphabet and the numbers 1–13. By the eighteenth century these elements were commonly included in samplers made in Great Britain, continental Europe, and the Americas. They served two functions: to introduce young girls to basic literacy and mathematics, and to teach them how to mark linens. In his *Treatise on the Education of Girls* (1687), François de Salignac La Mothe-Fénelon wrote that for women to fulfill their roles as housewives and mothers they should pursue a religious and moral education including reading, writing, basic mathematics, history, needlework, music, and Latin. The sampler helped fulfill at least three of Fénelon's goals.

Continental European samplers such as this German example usually included the alphabet and numbers, but more emphasis was placed on needlework skills than in contemporary British or American examples, which offered a narrower range of patterns and stitches.

Artist Unkown
Egyptian
Sampler fragment, Mamluk period,
1300–1420
17½ x 5⅞ in. (44.5 x 15 cm)
Plain weave linen embroidered with silk
Stitches: pattern darning
Harriet Otis Cruft Fund 48.1053

Origins

The earliest surviving samplers were excavated in Egypt and date from the Mamluk period (1250–1517). Professional embroiderers made them in order to provide clients with examples of the stitches, patterns, or colors available to ornament the seams and hems of linen shifts and sashes. Rectangular Mamluk samplers can today be found in a number of museum collections and are embroidered with the broad and narrow bands in pattern darning. In this technique, the embroidery thread is woven through the ground cloth from front to back, with pattern created when the thread floats over the surface. This narrow fragment of a sampler has patterns similar to those used on the ends of Mamluk waist sashes.

The dry climate of Egypt has fortunately preserved evidence of what must have been a much larger embroidery tradition that existed throughout the Mediterranean world. Sadly, it is not the same for European samplers, of which the earliest known evidence dates from the sixteenth century. Embroidery patterns similar to the Mamluks' for ornamenting linens became fashionable in fourteenth-century Italy and spread throughout Europe and Great Britain. The fashion reached its peak during the late fifteenth century, and it is shortly afterward that we find the first written and pictorial evidence for the use of samplers in Europe.

41

Pattern books

Sixty years after Johannes Gutenberg invented the printing press and published the first Bible, printers began to create pattern books for weavers and embroiderers. The earliest known pattern book, printed in 1523 by J. Schönsberger in Augsburg, Germany, contains woodblock prints of decorative borders for surface embroidery or pulled work (see W, p. 56). Schönsberger's book was followed by others produced in Germany, France, Italy, and Great Britain. One of the most influential pattern books, *Newes Modelbuch in Kupffer gemacht* (published by J. Sibmacher of Nuremberg in 1601), was often plagiarized and its designs have influenced embroidery up through the nineteenth century. This sampler was worked in Southern Germany in 1692. Several of the embroidered designs are found in late seventeenth-century pattern books published by Rosina Helena Fürst, the daughter of an art dealer and publisher. The central long-handled vase with three flowers appears in Fürst's *Model Buch*, along with several designs copied from Sibmacher's book, notably the peacock, stag, and hunting scene found in the third and fourth registers.

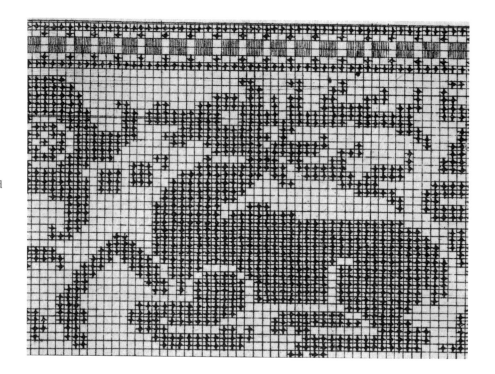

Artist Unkown
German

Sampler, 1692
18⅞ x 12⅛ in. (47.9 x 30.7 cm)
Plain weave linen embroidered in silk
Stitches: back, eyelet, running, satin, split, and two-sided Italian cross, buttonhole stitch edging
The Elizabeth Day McCormick Collection
43.979

Above: Detail from Johannes Sibmacher, *Schön neues Modelbuch* (Balthaser Caimox, Nuremberg, 1597), plate XVI.

43

Quatrain

This Needle Work Of Mine Can Tell
When A Child Is Learned Well
That By My Elders I Was Taught
Not To Spend My Time For Naught

Mary Burges embroidered this quatrain
into her sampler of 1725. It is the earliest
known sampler from Rhode Island and is
similar to another by Hannah Hoockey
from 1728 (Newport Historical Society).
Both samplers closely resemble those
made in England at the end of the seventeenth century, when Bible verses and
moral sayings were added to the repetitive
borders. Mary Burges's verse reveals senti-
ments common to the early-eighteenth
century: filial duty and industry.

Mary Burges

American, Rhode Island, born about 1715

Sampler, 1725
16⁹/₁₆ x 7³/₁₆ in. (42.6 x 19.7 cm)
Plain weave linen embroidered in silk
Stitches: cross, double-running, eyelet, long-
armed cross, Montenegrin cross, and satin
Gift of Miss Florence R. Kenyon 45.763

R

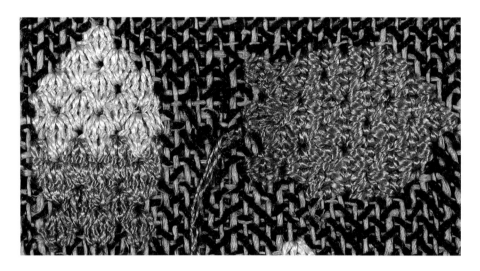

Rococo stitch

The samplers worked by the Providence schoolteacher Mary Balch's students are not only exceptional because of their imaginative designs, but employ an astonishing range of stitches. Rococo stitch, not often seen in samplers as of the seventeenth and early eighteenth centuries (see S, p. 48), was used by Betsy Davis to fill in the flowers and strawberries ornamenting the borders. Rococo stitch, a canvaswork stitch worked over four yarns of the ground fabric, leaves an openwork structure similar to pulled work.

Betsy Davis
American, Providence, Rhode Island

Sampler, 1796
17 ½ x 14 ½ in. (44.5 x 36.8 cm) including frame
Plain weave linen embroidered in silk
Stitches: chain, cross, diagonal, rococo, satin, shaded satin, and tent
Gift of Mr. Gilbert Russell Payson and Mr. Henry G. E. Payson 45.767

Spot sampler

Spot samplers are samplers with embroidered motifs randomly scattered over the surface. They were used by both professional embroiderers and amateur needlewomen to collect patterns and stitches for reference. This British sampler from the early seventeenth century, made by an amateur needlewoman, shows a collection of designs and stitches suitable for use on household embroideries and personal objects. The geometric motifs on the left can often be found ornamenting small bags, and the flowers and insects created in tent stitch on the right, known as "slips," were embroidered, cut out, and appliquéd to domestic furnishings such as bed hangings and cushion covers.

Artist Unknown
British

Spot sampler, about 1600–1650
18⅜ x 15¾ in. (46.7 x 40 cm)
Plain weave linen embroidered with silk and metallic thread
Stitches: back, cross, eye, eyelet, marking cross, reverse chain, reverse tent, rococo, Rumanian, satin, and tent; pulled work including faggot; metallic thread embroidered in looped and interlaced stitches including heavy chain, interlacing knots, and plaited braid
Gift of Mrs. Samuel Cabot and Mrs. J. Templeton Coolidge 33.667

Trade sampler

Trade samplers were used by professional embroiderers to demonstrate their skill and to illustrate the available designs and stitches. This sampler was embroidered in a style known as "Ayrshire work," which developed in Scotland in the early nineteenth century. Inspired by the finely embroidered accessories of the eighteenth century (see W, p. 56), Ayrshire work was characterized by cutwork (see I, p. 28) with needle lace fillings and embroidery in satin stitch. It was especially popular for use on christening caps and robes, but can also be found on women's clothing and accessories.

Artist Unknown
Scottish, Ayrshire

Trade sampler, about 1825–1850
20 ¹¹⁄₁₆ x 24 ⅝ in. (52.5 x 62.5 cm)
Cotton plain weave embroidered in cotton
Stitches: chain (from the back), padded satin, satin, and whipped stem; cutwork with various fillings
Gift of Philip Lehman in memory of his wife Carrie L. Lehman 38.1132

Artist Unknown

Possibly German

Spot sampler, 1669
20⅞ x 25 3/16 in. (53 x 64.3 cm)
Plain weave linen embroidered in silk, wool,
metallic thread, and purl loops; glass beads
Stitches: couching, rococo, and tent
The Elizabeth Day McCormick Collection
43.289

Umlaut

In working with historic objects, there are
always several that do not fit into accepted
categories. Many contain recognizable
elements that would appear to help place
them chronologically and geographically,
but they also contain others that force us
to rethink our current understanding of
the material. This seventeenth-century
sampler is one such example. At first
glance it looks typical of early to mid
seventeenth-century English spot samplers, with its scattered geometric patterns
and tent stitch flowers, birds, and animals
(see S, p. 48). Other elements, however,
are less easy to place: the presence of the
Virgin Mary and child, as well as Saint
Catherine, tell us immediately that this
sampler was worked not by a Protestant
girl but by a Catholic; the initials MAÖ
are not English, because of the umlaut
over the *o*; and unlike English spot samplers, the ground is completely covered
in tent stitch. These elements suggest a
German origin, specifically from the
southern part of the country. But where
the sampler was in fact made and by
whom will remain a mystery unless more
samplers like it with better documenta-
tion are found.

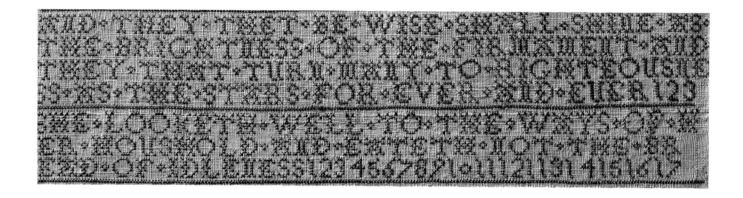

Sarah Barnett
British

Marking Sampler, 1738
12 ⁹⁄₁₆ x 8 ¹¹⁄₁₆ in. (32.5 x 22 cm)
Plain weave linen embroidered with silk
Stitches: cross, eyelet
Gift of Mrs. F. H. Cook 39.566

Verse

In samplers, as in literature, verse can refer to a line of poetry or a passage from the Bible. Both kinds of verses were added to samplers during the seventeenth century as embroidery was incorporated into the female curriculum. Memorization was a key element in learning, and Dr. Isaac Watts (1674–1748), one of the most influential writers of hymns in the early eighteenth century, wrote in the preface to his *Divine and Moral Songs for Children* (1720) that "what is learned in verse is longer retained in memory and sooner recollected." Sarah Barnett in her 1738 sampler has copied a series of verses from the Bible, several of which relate to a woman's role as homemaker. From *Proverbs,* Chapter 31, Verse 13, she embroidered, "She looketh well to the ways of her houshold and eateth not the bread of idleness." Also from *Proverbs,* Chapter 31, she chose Verse 15: "She riseth also while it is yet night and giveth meat to her houshold and a porsion to her maidens."

Bible verses provided plenty of opportunity for Sarah Barnett to practice her marking skills. Initials, for example, were often embroidered into linens to indicate ownership, while crowns or coronets (such as the ones at the bottom of Sarah's sampler) were used by aristocratic families to denote noble rank.

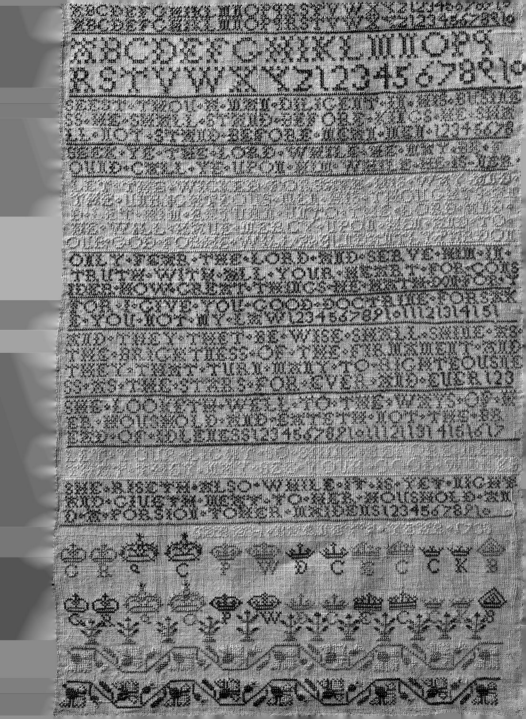

cm)
oidered with linen

, cross, satin, and
ncluding eyelet, hem,
titches
Croft, "Gardner
6279

Whitework is a general term used to iden-tify white thread embroidery on a white ground. The embroidery can be done with simple stitches, such as satin and stem, or with more complicated tech-niques, such as cutwork or pulled work. Pulled work (or drawn work, as it is known in Britain) is created by displacing the warp and weft threads of the ground cloth with high-tension embroidery. The holes created in the ground resemble lace. In cutwork, a section of the ground or individual threads are cut away and filled in, usually with buttonhole stitching or one of its variations.

Whitework embroidery incorporating pulled work became especially popular during the eighteenth century as a cheap-er substitute for lace. By the middle of the century, lightweight lace with the feel of muslin was in high fashion and whitework made an effective substitute. It was made throughout Europe and even in the American colonies, but the best white-work came from Southern Germany. Dresden became the center of its trade and the town's name is now associated with a particularly finely patterned white-on-white embroidery. This sampler was probably made in Southern Germany and shows the quality of the linen used and the variety of filling patterns that could be achieved. The lower register illustrates how the different filling patterns were combined to create delicate floral designs.

Jane Atkinson

English, Whitby, Yorkshire, born 1768

Sampler, about 1780
18⅛ x 13³⁄₁₆ in. (46.1 x 33.5 cm)
Plain weave wool embroidered with silk
Stitches: back, cross, and satin
The Elizabeth Day McCormick Collection
43.284

X-stitch

Cross stitch, which is quickly executed and covers large areas of canvas effectively, was well suited to the samplers of the later eighteenth and nineteenth centuries. By this time, education for girls had spread throughout the middle class. Girls like Jane Atkinson, whose father was a sailor out of the port of Whitby, Yorkshire, would have had less time for the fancywork of the past, but instead would have been given a more practical education. Jane's sampler, with its seemingly elaborate border, could have been quickly worked in cross stitch and brought home as a symbol of her accomplishments.

Artist Unknown
German

Sampler, 1805
25 x 15 in. (63.5 x 38 cm)
Silk plain weave embroidered with silk,
metallic yarn, coils, and paillettes
Stitches: chain, couching, French knot, running, shaded satin, satin, and stem
The Elizabeth Day McCormick Collection
43.952

Yarn

A yarn is an assemblage of fibers or fila-
ments put together to create a continuous
strand. The amount of spin used to bind
the fibers can affect the strength, luster,
and elasticity of the yarn. The fiber also
has great impact on the final product.
This sampler exploits the characteristics
of silk yarns, which are made by unwind-
ing long strands of silk filament and com-
bining them to create thicker yarns suitable for weaving or embroidery. The long,
unbroken strands of filament are what
give silk its high luster and strength. The
girl who embroidered this sampler has
taken advantage of the reflective quality
of silk by her use of satin stitch, resulting
in long strands of silk yarn. Metallic
threads embroidered into the sampler
provide an example of complex yarns, in
which two or more different elements are
spun together. In this case, silk is used to
create a strong core, while the silver metal
strips add sparkle.

Z

Artist Unknown
Probably German

Band Sampler, early 1800s
30⅛ x 12¼ in. (76.5 x 31.1 cm)
Plain weave wool embroidered with silk
Stitches: tent
The Elizabeth Day McCormick Collection
43.982

Z-twist

The letter Z is used to designate yarns that have been spun or plied clockwise, or from right to left. For yarns twisted counter-clockwise, or from left to right, the letter S is used. In Egypt, linen fibers have been traditionally spun in the S-direction, which can be seen in examples going back to the Dynastic period. Linen fibers twist slightly in the same direction, and by spinning them together counter-clockwise a strong, more tightly spun thread is achieved. The tradition of spinning in the Z-direction developed in Europe and India and has persisted to this day, as can be seen in the yarns used to form the grounds in most of the samplers illustrated in this book.

The cream-colored ground of this nineteenth-century sampler is made of Z-spun wool yarns. Wool canvas was used often during the eighteenth and nineteenth centuries in English, German, and Danish samplers. The silk yarns embroidered onto the wool ground were spun in the opposite, or S, direction.

Bibliography

Abegg, Margaret. *Apropos Patterns for Embroidery, Lace and Woven Textiles.* Bern: Abegg-Stiftung, 1978.

Baker, Patricia L. *Islamic Textiles.* London: British Museum Press, 1995.

Barber, Elizabeth Wayland. *Prehistoric Textiles.* Princeton, New Jersey: Princeton University Press, 1991.

Button, H. Warren, and Eugene F. Provenzo, Jr. *History of Education & Culture in America.* 2nd ed. Englewood Cliffs, New Jersey: Prentice Hall, 1989.

Christie, Mrs. Archibald. *Samplers and Stitches: A Handbook of the Embroiderer's Art.* 3rd ed. London: B. T. Batsford Ltd., 1934.

Colby, Averil. *Samplers.* 2nd ed. London: B. T. Batsford Ltd., 1984.

Garrett, Elisabeth Donaghy. Theodore Mitchell, and Heather Caldwell. *Lessons Stitched in Silk: Samplers from the Canterbury Region of New Hampshire.* Dartmouth, New Hampshire: Hood Museum of Art, Dartmouth College, 1990.

Humphrey, Carol. *Samplers.* Cambridge: Cambridge University Press, 1997.

King, Donald. *Samplers.* London: Victoria and Albert Museum, 1960.

Levey, Santina M. *Lace: A History.* London: Victoria & Albert Museum and W. S. Maney & Son Limited, 1993.

Morris, Barbara. *Victorian Embroidery.* London: Herbert Jenkins, 1962.

Moss, Gillian. *Embroidered Samplers in the Collection of the Cooper-Hewitt Museum.* Washington, DC: The Smithsonian Institution, 1984.

Pulliam, John D. *History of Education in America.* 4th ed. Columbus, Ohio: Merrill Publishing Company, 1987.

Ring, Betty. *Girlhood Embroidery: American Samplers & Pictorial Needlework 1650–1850.* 2 vols. New York: Alfred A. Knopf, 1993.

Ring, Betty. *Let Virtue Be a Guide to Thee: Needlework in the Education of Rhode Island Women, 1730-1780.* Providence: The Rhode Island Historical Society, 1983.

Swain, Margaret. *Scottish Embroidery Medieval to Modern.* London: B. T. Batsford Ltd., 1986.

Wanner-Jean Richard, Anne. *Patterns and Motifs: Catalogue of Samplers, St. Gallen Textile Museum.* St. Gallen: VGS Verlagsgemeinschaft St. Gallen, 1996.